ANDREW LLOYD WEBBER™

GOLD

ISBN 0-634-04969-0

HAL•LEONARD®
CORPORATION
7777 W. BLUEMOUND RD. P.O. BOX 13819 MILWAUKEE, WI 53213

Andrew Lloyd Webber™ is a trademark owned by Andrew Lloyd Webber

Visit Hal Leonard Online at
www.halleonard.com

SUPERSTAR
from JESUS CHRIST SUPERSTAR

Words by TIM RICE
Music by ANDREW LLOYD WEBBER

As If We Never Said Goodbye

from SUNSET BOULEVARD

Music by ANDREW LLOYD WEBBER
Lyrics by DON BLACK and CHRISTOPHER HAMPTON,
with contributions by Amy Powers

THE PHANTOM OF THE OPERA
from THE PHANTOM OF THE OPERA

Music by ANDREW LLOYD WEBBER
Lyrics by CHARLES HART
Additional Lyrics by RICHARD STILGOE and MIKE BATT

CHRISTINE: In sleep he sang to me, _____ in dreams he came,

YOU MUST LOVE ME
from the Cinergi Motion Picture EVITA

Words by TIM RICE
Music by ANDREW LLOYD WEBBER

Flowing

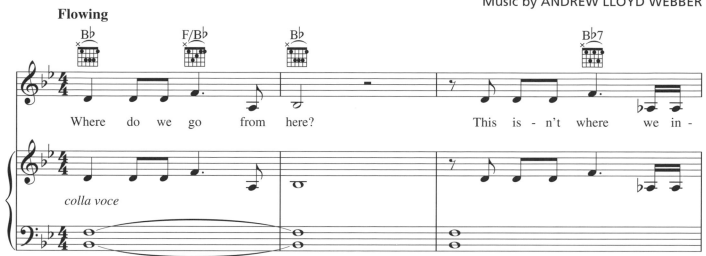

Where do we go from here? This is - n't where we in -

tend - ed to be. __ We had it all, __ you be - lieved __ in me, __ I be -

lieved __ in you. __

Cer - tain - ties dis - ap -
Why are you at my

ANY DREAM WILL DO

from JOSEPH AND THE AMAZING TECHNICOLOR DREAMCOAT

Music by ANDREW LLOYD WEBBER
Lyrics by TIM RICE

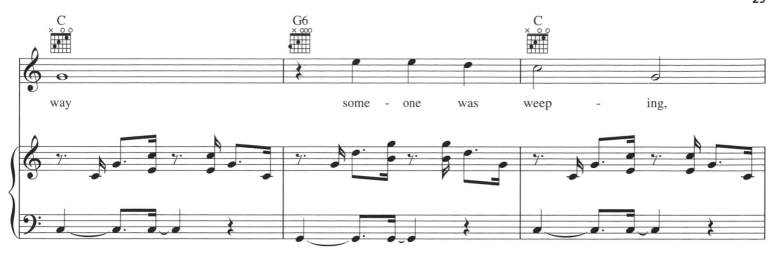

way   some-one was weep - ing,

but the world was sleep - ing,   an - y dream will

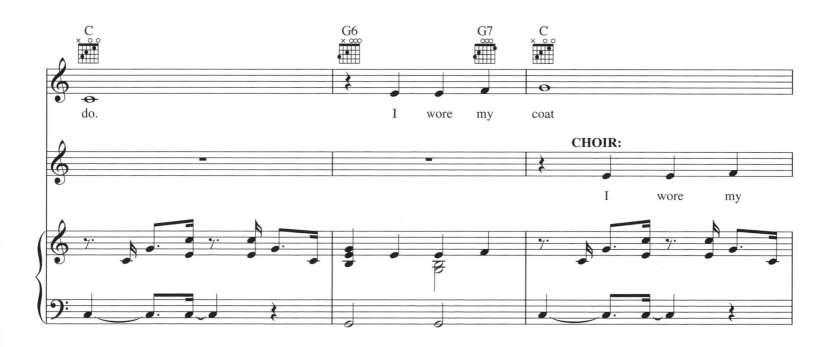

do.   I wore my coat

CHOIR:

I wore my

MEMORY
from CATS

Music by ANDREW LLOYD WEBBER
Text by TREVOR NUNN after T.S. ELIOT

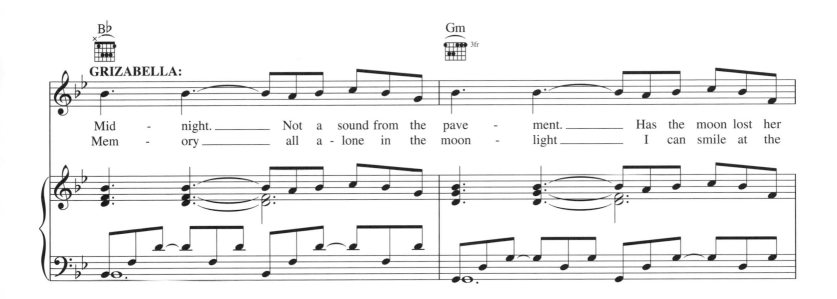

Burnt out ends of smo - ky days, ___ the stale cold smell ___ of

PIE JESU
from REQUIEM

By ANDREW LLOYD WEBBER

re - qui - em.

SOLO BOY: *mp*

Pi - e Je - su, _____ pi - e Je - su, _____ pi - e

Qui tol - lis pec - ca - ta mun - di,

Je - su, _____ pi - e Je - su, Qui tol - lis pec - ca - ta mun - di,

SOPRANO

ALTO

Hm _____

TENOR

BASS

THE MUSIC OF THE NIGHT
from THE PHANTOM OF THE OPERA

Music by ANDREW LLOYD WEBBER
Lyrics by CHARLES HART
Additional Lyrics by RICHARD STILGOE

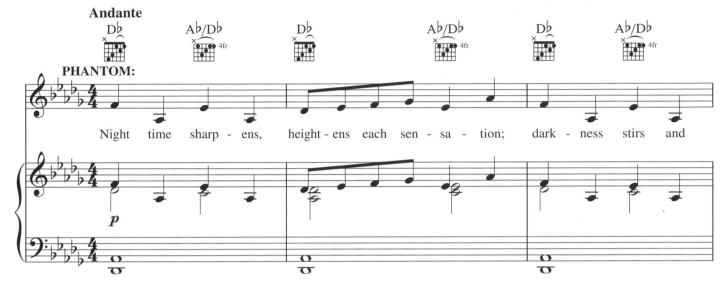

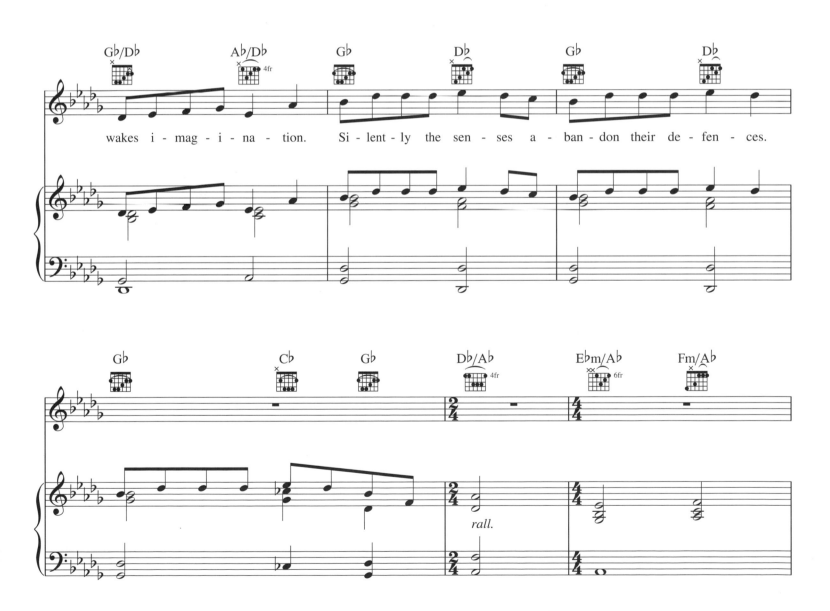

Float - ing, fall - ing, sweet in - tox - i - ca - tion. Touch me, trust me,

sa - vour each sen - sa - tion. Let the dream be - gin, let your dark - er side give in to the

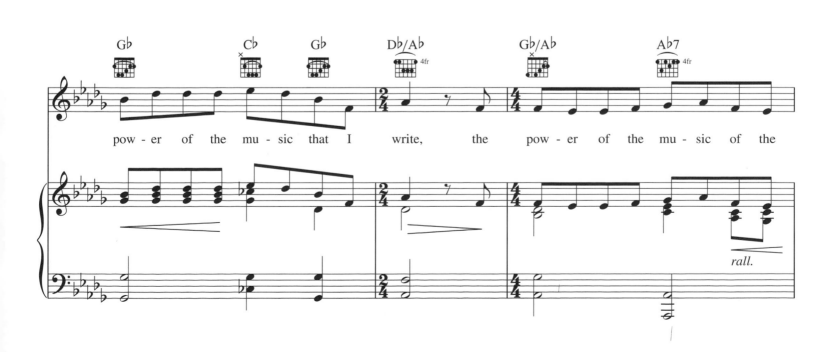

pow - er of the mu - sic that I write, the pow - er of the mu - sic of the

I DON'T KNOW HOW TO LOVE HIM

from JESUS CHRIST SUPERSTAR

Words by TIM RICE
Music by ANDREW LLOYD WEBBER

DON'T CRY FOR ME ARGENTINA

from EVITA

Words by TIM RICE
Music by ANDREW LLOYD WEBBER

look at me to know that ev-'ry word is true. ___

LOVE CHANGES EVERYTHING
from ASPECTS OF LOVE

Music by ANDREW LLOYD WEBBER
Lyrics by DON BLACK and CHARLES HART

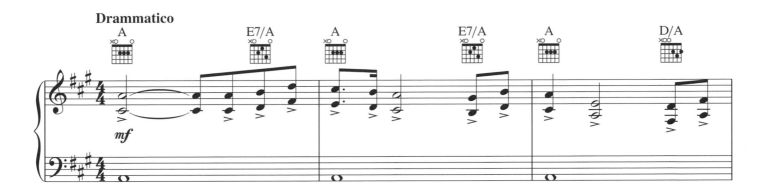

Love, love chang-es ev-'ry-thing: hands and
Love, love chang-es ev-'ry-thing: days are

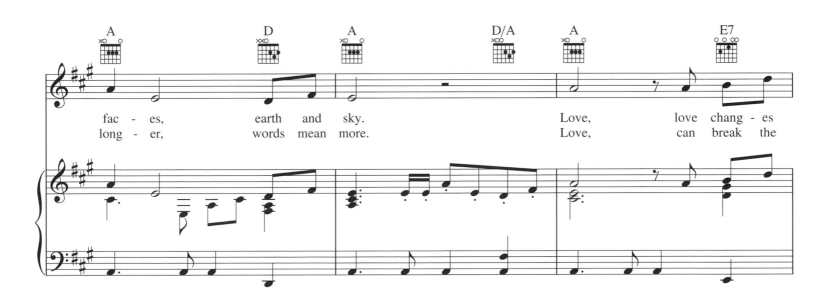

fac-es, earth and sky. Love, love chang-es
long-er, words mean more. Love, can break the

ALL I ASK OF YOU

from THE PHANTOM OF THE OPERA

Music by ANDREW LLOYD WEBBER
Lyrics by CHARLES HART
Additional Lyrics by RICHARD STILGOE

No more talk of dark - ness, for - get these wide - eyed fears: I'm

here, noth - ing can harm you, my words will warm and calm you.

Let me be your free - dom, let day - light dry your tears: I'm

74

THE PERFECT YEAR
from SUNSET BOULEVARD

Music by ANDREW LLOYD WEBBER
Lyrics by DON BLACK and CHRISTOPHER HAMPTON

Moderato

mp

simile

NORMA:

Ring out the old, ring in the new, a mid-night

wish to share with you. Your lips are warm, my head is light, were we a-

live be-fore to-night? I don't need a crowd-ed

THE VAULTS OF HEAVEN

from WHISTLE DOWN THE WIND

Music by ANDREW LLOYD WEBBER
Lyrics by JIM STEINMAN

NO MATTER WHAT

from WHISTLE DOWN THE WIND

Music by ANDREW LLOYD WEBBER
Lyrics by JIM STEINMAN

OH WHAT A CIRCUS

from EVITA

Words by TIM RICE
Music by ANDREW LLOYD WEBBER

Additional Lyrics

2. Oh, what an exit! That's how to go!
   When they're ringing your curtain down
   Demand to be buried like Eva Peron.
   It's quite a sunset
   And good for the country in a roundabout way
   We've made the front pages of all the world's papers today!

3. Salve regina, mater misericordiae,
   Vita dulcedo et spes nostra.
   Salve, salve regina,
   Ad te clamamus exules filii Eva,
   Ad te suspiramus gementes et flentes
   O clemens, O pia!

4. She had her moments, she had some style.
   The best show in town was the crowd
   Outside the Casa Rosada crying "Eva Peron."
   But that's all gone now
   As soon as the smoke from the funeral clears
   We're all going to see - and how! - she did nothing for years.
   You let down your people Evita
   You were supposed to have been immortal
   That's all they wanted
   Not much to ask for
   But in the end you could not deliver.

5. Salve regina, mater misericordiae,
   Vita dulcedo et spes nostra.
   Salve, salve regina,
   Ad te clamamus exules filii Eva,
   Ad te suspiramus gementes et flentes
   O clemens, O pia! (Repeat)

WHISTLE DOWN THE WIND

from WHISTLE DOWN THE WIND

Music by ANDREW LLOYD WEBBER
Lyrics by JIM STEINMAN

AMIGOS PARA SIEMPRE
(Friends for Life)
The Official Theme of the Barcelona 1992 Games

Music by ANDREW LLOYD WEBBER
Lyrics by DON BLACK

I _____ don't have to say a word to you, _____ you seem to know what-ev-er
We _____ share mem-o-ries I won't for-get. _____ And we'll share more, my friend, we

mood I'm go-ing through. Feel as though I've known you for-ev - er.
have-n't start-ed yet. Some-thing hap-pens when we're to-geth - er.